I0013842

THE FOUR HOUR SERIES

THE 4 HOUR EXCEL GUIDE

FOR THE BUSY IT GUY

Maxxwell Cooper

THE 4 HOUR EXCEL GUIDE FOR THE BUSY IT GUY

THE 4 HOUR SERIES

Copyright © 2018 Maxxwell Cooper

www.maxxwellcooper.com

ISBN: 9781983265754

First Published on Amazon

Cover (illustration) by Maxxwell Cooper

All rights reserved. No part of this publication may be reproduced, stored in or introduced into a retrieval system, or transmitted, in any form, or by any means (electrical, mechanical, photocopying, recording or otherwise) without the prior written permission of the author. Any person who does any unauthorized act in relation to this publication may be liable to criminal prosecution and civil claims for damages.

Dedicated to my parents.

Their love and blessings always inspire me to keep Going!!!

CONTENTS

INTRODUCTION

Microsoft Excel has been an integral part of most of our daily tasks at work. Being an IT Engineer myself, I have always been fascinated with the unending functionalities and capabilities in this piece of software. I never realized that Microsoft Excel and PowerPoint would become my bread and butter, especially when I transitioned into a managerial role.

Being in IT, striking a balance between work and family has itself been an imperative for me. Taking out time to learn new things on top of it has been a challenge in itself. I really wished there could have been an easy way out to learn the key features to get me ahead of the game.

Having been asked innumerable number of times by my friends and colleagues at the office in helping them with Excel, inspired me to write this book. It certainly aims at resolving a lot of those concerns.

This self-paced book aims to help you get you kick started on some of the key features in Microsoft Excel, all in a weekend read! In contrast to bulky manuals, this book serves the purpose of learning key features which will help you get that extra edge while working in Excel.

So, without taking much time, I thank you for purchasing the book and let's get on with the quick learning.

Here's Wishing You Good Luck for a Great Career!!!

Maxxwell Cooper

CHAPTER 01
LIST MANGEMENT

LIST MANGEMENT

Lists are the main source of our data. Handling and formatting lists is an important step towards extracting useful information out of our data.

In this chapter, we begin with basic sorting of lists followed by learning how to use filters. We will also learn how to freeze panes so we can reference useful columns while scrolling through the data.

SORTING

Let us start with taking a sample list given below with three easy columns containing marks of a student in different subjects.

Sr. No.	Subject	Marks
1	English	85
2	Maths	67
3	Physics	54
4	Chemistry	68
5	Biology	79

Let us sort this list in order of increasing marks.

Steps:

1) Click anywhere on the Table (make sure each

column has headers mentioned. For example, Sr. No., Subject, Marks).

2) Click on "DATA" Tab, then on "Sort" Button which produces the following Dialogue Box.

This step can also be performed via a simple shortcut of Alt+D => S.

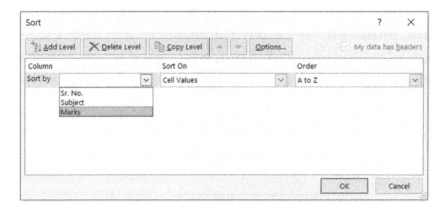

3) Here you can click on the Drop-Down menu against "Sort By" as shown in the picture above.

- Choose the respective header of the field you wish you sort the data by and then choose ascending (A to Z) or descending (Z to A) order under the "Order" Drop-Down menu.

4) You can sort the data using multiple fields.

- Click on "Add Level" to add a second sorting criteria.
- You can choose to change the order of execution of these criteria using the Up

and Down arrows.
- Finally, Click "OK".

5) There is an additional option in the above picture that not many know of.

- If you click on "Options...," you can choose to decide the Orientation of sorting.

- Most common practice is to sort from Top to Bottom.
- But you can use this option to sort the data from Left to Right as well.
- You will also notice an additional option if you wish to sort the data as "Case Sensitive."

DATA FILTERS

Filters are a great option to dynamically navigate through the data. We can choose different permutations and combinations to effectively dig out the list of data we are looking for.

For example: The table besides provides the export figures for Apple and Oranges by ABC Corp. in 2016 and 2017.

Sr. No.	Item	Quantity	Year	Quarter
1	Apple	10000	2016	Jan-Mar
2	Orange	5000	2016	Jan-Mar
3	Apple	14000	2016	Apr-Jun
4	Orange	7000	2016	Apr-Jun
5	Apple	13000	2016	Jul-Sep
6	Orange	6000	2016	Jul-Sep
7	Apple	9000	2016	Oct-Dec
8	Orange	4000	2016	Oct-Dec
9	Apple	9000	2017	Jan-Mar
10	Orange	6000	2017	Jan-Mar
11	Apple	13000	2017	Apr-Jun
12	Orange	8000	2017	Apr-Jun
13	Apple	12000	2017	Jul-Sep
14	Orange	7000	2017	Jul-Sep
15	Apple	10000	2017	Oct-Dec
16	Orange	5000	2017	Oct-Dec

What if we have to compare the performance of Apple exports for the Jan-Mar Quarter between 2016 and 2017?

No worries!

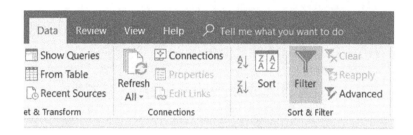

- For this, we need to first enable the Filters.
- To activate Filters, Click anywhere on the Table, then click on "DATA" followed by "Filter" button.

This can also be accomplished by keyboard shortcut "ALT+D => F => F".

- You can use the same combination to toggle between activation and deactivation of the filters.
- Once the Filter is enabled, click on the Filter Drop-down menu against "Item" Column and Select "Apple."
- Similarly, in the Filter Drop-down menu for the "Quarter" Column, select "Jan-Mar."

Sr. No. ▼	Item �ﾏ	Quantity ▼	Year ▼	Quarter �ﾏ
1	Apple	10000	2016	Jan-Mar
9	Apple	9000	2017	Jan-Mar

The resultant will be like the table shown in the picture above. This is how filters make it easy for us to compare various permutations and combinations of the data.

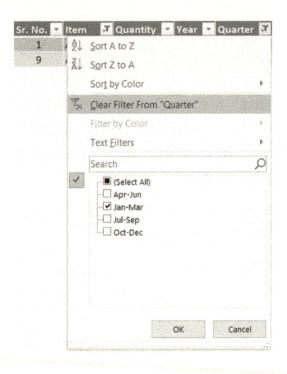

As a next exercise, you can select the Quarters in which the sale of Oranges was greater than or equal to 7000.

- ❖ Before we can do this, we need to clear the previously selected filters.
- ❖ This could be done by reversing the steps performed above.
- ❖ Alternatively, we can go to respective Filter's Drop-down menu and choose

"Clear Filter from "Item"."

❖ This will automatically clear the filter set for that particular column.

❖ This step needs to be repeated for every column where we have selected filters.

❖ To identify which columns have Filters selected, you will notice the Filter sign in the Filter Drop-down menu instead of an inverted triangle.

Sr. No. ▼	Item ⏍	Quantity ▼	Year ▼	Quarter ⏍
1	Apple	10000	2016	Jan-Mar
9	Apple	9000	2017	Jan-Mar

❖ You can save time by clearing all filters at once by clicking on "DATA" followed by "Filter" and "Clear."

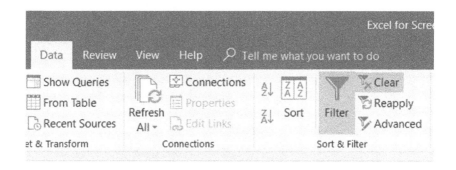

Text/Number Filters:

Text Filters are great option when you have to

select data as per any criteria.

- You will get option for "Text Filters" in Filter Drop-down menu of a Column containing Text
- Similarly, "Number Filters" appear while working on Filter Drop-down menu of field containing numbers only.

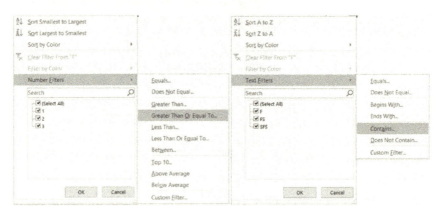

- You need to choose the respective criteria in the next window and then Click "OK."

FREEZE PANES

While performing data analysis in a table with large number of Columns, it becomes difficult to refer values against data present in the initial columns.

As we scroll towards right, the initial columns also scroll towards left and disappear from the view.

A quick solution to this is to use the "Freeze Panes" option in Excel.

- To enable this, we need to click on the Cell from where we want to freeze the data, then click "View" => "Freeze Panes."
- You also have the option to choose to freeze the "Top Row" or the "First Column" individually.

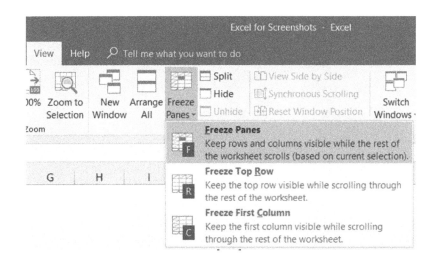

- The Keyboard shortcut to this will be "ALT+W" => "F" => "F."
- You can repeat the same steps/shortcut to toggle between activating and deactivating the "Freeze Panes" option.
- Please note that when you enable the "Freeze Panes" option, the rows present on the left side of the cell in focus as well as the rows present above will freeze and not disappear as we continue to scroll towards the right or bottom of the spreadsheet.

CHAPTER 02
CONDITIONAL FORMATTING

CONDITIONAL FORMATTING

Conditional formatting helps in highlighting cells in different colors based on the criteria we define. We can have one or more criteria.

In the Example below, a Table displaying the scores of five students in the subject of Science is presented.

Sr. No.	Name	Marks
1	Max	85
2	Tabetha	75
3	Bill	95
4	Susan	59
5	Mary	64

If we were to highlight the students who have attained 75 or more marks in science, we need to make use of Conditional Formatting.

Steps:

1) Select the Cells on which you want to apply Conditional Formatting.

2) Click on "HOME" Tab, followed by "Conditional Formatting" button and then "Mange Rules".

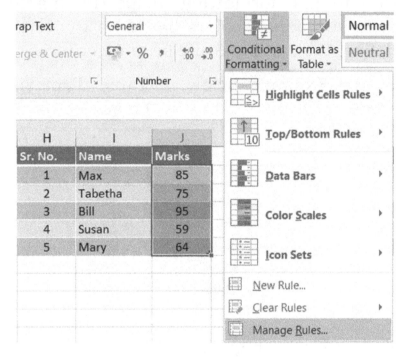

- Here you could have chosen "New Rule" option instead of "Manage Rules" if you had to create a single rule.
- The latter is used while creating multiple rules.
- This opens the "Conditional Formatting Rules Manger" Dialog Box.

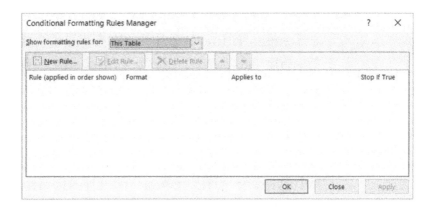

3) Click on "New Rule" which opens the "New Formatting Rule" Dialog Box as shown below:

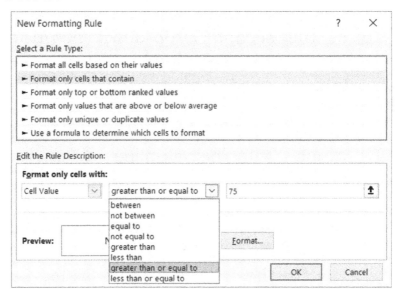

- This Dialog Box provides us six ways to decide the criteria selection.
- The most common option used is the last one called "Format only cells that

contain."

- This option enables you to choose criteria based on cell value, choose blank or non-blank cells specifically, or even choose cells which contain or do not contain an error.
- This way Excel can easily decide to activate the color highlighting whenever the result of the formula is TRUE.

4) In the first Drop-down menu choose "Cell Value" which is usually the default value.

5) In the second Drop-down menu choose "Greater than or equal to" and in the third box you need to enter the value "75."

6) Next step is to choose the Cell formatting which will be applied whenever the formula/condition becomes TRUE.

7) Click on the "Format" Button on the "New Formatting Rule" Dialog Box.
   - In the "Format Cells" Dialog Box you get the option to format the Cell Color (using "Fill" Tab), change the Font, format the Border of the cell, or change the presentation of the Text value (using "Number" Tab).

- The most common ones used are the Fill Tab and the Font Tab which help us in highlighting the cell with a distinct color and also provide a different font (we could change to Bold or Italics and Underline; even choose a combination of these). We can also change the Font being used in the affected cell).
- Select the changes you want to apply to the affected cells and Click "OK" twice to go back to the "Conditional Formatting Rules Manager."

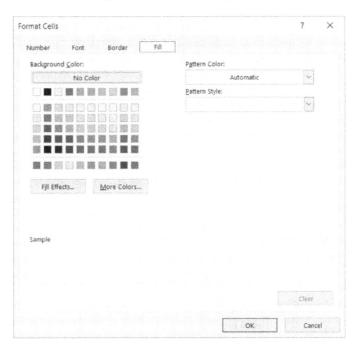

8) Now that you have successfully created one Rule, you can choose to Click "Apply"

and then "OK."

- Alternatively, you can create another rule by clicking on "New Rule" and follow the steps above to create a new rule.

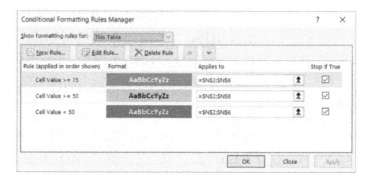

- Repeat these steps multiple times depending upon the number of criteria you want to create.
- You can also change the order of execution by clicking the Up (button with triangle symbol) and Down (button with inverted triangle symbol) buttons.
- You can also choose to stop the execution of the order whenever the criteria is met, else Excel will continue to process other rules as well.
- The Table below shows what the result is going to be for the table

discussed above.

Sr. No.	Name	Marks
1	Max	85
2	Tabetha	75
3	Bill	95
4	Susan	59
5	Mary	64

- Click "OK" once done.

CHAPTER 03
DATA VALIDATION

DATA VALIDATION

Data Validation is a great tool when you want to prevent the user from entering an invalid type of data.

For example:

- If we want the user to enter a number in a certain field, which is and that number also is used in a formula.
- In this case, if the user mistakenly types in a text or a character other than numbers, the calculation shows up as error.
- If we put in a mechanism that restricts the user from entering anything else except a number only, it will save us a lot of effort.

Let us do a simple exercise:

- We take an example of the table below in which each student is required to enter their details such as Name, Roll No. and Class.

Sr. No.	Name	Roll No.	Class
1			
2			
3			

- While the fields Name and Class can have text, it is a requirement that only numbers should be entered in the Roll No. field. Please follow the following to enable this.

We follow the steps below, in order to make sure that only numbers are entered in the Roll No. Section (Column):

1) Select all the cells under "Roll No." field where the entries need to be made.
2) Click on "DATA" Tab, then "Data Validation" button, which will bring the "Data Validation" Dialog Box as shown below.

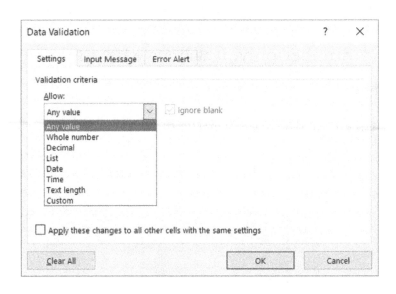

3) The picture above shows the various options available in the "Allow" Drop-down

menu in the "Settings" Tab, the default being "Any value."

4) Since, we want to restrict the user to only enter a number without digits, we need to choose the option "Decimal."

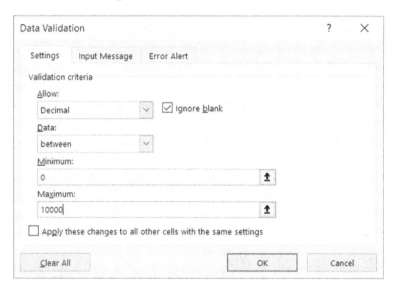

5) Next, we can also restrict the minimum and/or maximum values if we want to, else you can leave them blank.

6) Here we choose to keep the values between 0 and 10000 as shown in the picture above.

7) Click "OK." Now try to enter any text into any of the fields under the "Roll No." and

you will receive the following default message.

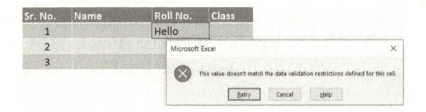

8) The "Data Validation" also provides two very helpful features called "Input Message" and "Error Alert."

9) Input Message: You would have seen, when you hover the mouse cursor over a field, it displays a small pop-up giving details or instructions.

10) To enable this, go back to the "Data Validation" Dialog Box. Then, Click on "Input Message" Tab, enter a title for your pop-up window in the "Title" field and enter a message in the "Input Message" field as displayed in the screenshot below.

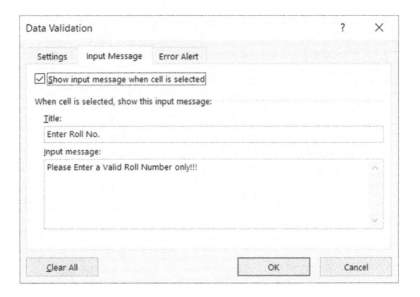

11) Click "OK." Now try moving the mouse cursor over any of the field under "Roll No." and it will display the message you just configured.

12) **Error Alert:** You can also customize the Error window shown to pass on corrective message to the user so the user can quickly enter the desired type of value.

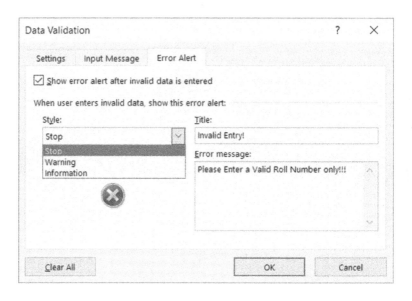

Sr. No.	Name	Roll No.	Class
1			
2			
3			

Enter Roll No.
Please Enter a
Valid Roll Number
only!!!

- It's all about user experience after all!
- To enable this, go back to the "Data Validation" Dialog Box, Click on "Error Alert" Tab.
- In the "Style" Drop-down menu, you have the option to decide what action needs to be taken.
- Should the user be stopped from making an entry, or should you just warn them or inform them about the mistake.

- The most commonly used option is to use the "Stop" option, which will not allow the user to enter an invalid type of data.
- You need to mention the relevant alert information in the "Title" and "Error Message" fields.

13)   Click "OK." Now, try to enter any non-number data into any cell under the "Roll No." field and it will give the error message as per the screenshot below.

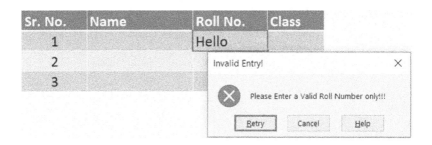

CHAPTER 04
IMPLEMENTING COMPLEX FORMULAE

IMPLEMENTING COMPLEX FORMULAE

In this chapter we will be using some of the Logical functions which help us deciding values based on the pre-existing conditions/values.

USING THE "IF" FUNCTION

The "IF" function is used to test a condition and decide what to execute based on the outcome of the condition as TRUE or FALSE.

❖ IF Function is divided into three parts:

IF (PART 1, PART2, PART3)

❖ PART1 contains the condition which when TRUE will return the value calculated by expression in PART2.
❖ If the condition in PART1 returns a FALSE will return the value calculated by expression in PART3.

Let us take the following example:

A store is selling premium apples at a 10% discount, if customers buy a minimum of two Kilos.

Item	Qty (Kg)	Discount Applicable? (Yes/No)	Rate ($)	Total
APPLES PREMIUM	5	Yes	$3.00	$13.50

- In the table above, we have used the IF formula in two cells C2 and E2.
- The table below shows the formula in each cell.

Item	Qty (Kg)	Discount Applicable? (Yes/No)	Rate ($)	Total
APPLES PREMIUM	5	=IF(B2>=2,"Yes","No")	3	=B2*D2*IF(B2>=2,90%,100%)

Let us try to understand both the formulas one by one:

Cell C2: =IF(B2>=2,"Yes","No")

PART1: B2>=2 :

- This formula returns a TRUE whenever the value of B2 (Quantity in Kg) is greater than or equal to 2.
- Hence, this IF formula will return a text (because of the double quotes around the words Yes and No) Yes if the Quantity (B2)

[38]

is greater than or equal to 2, or a No if the Quantity (B2) is less than 2.

- The overall resultant value tells the user whether the discount is applicable or not based on the quantity entered in cell B2.

Cell E2: =B2*D2*IF(B2>=2,90%,100%)

Let us first examine the IF expression here **IF(B2>=2,90%,100%)**

PART1: B2>=2 :

- This formula returns a TRUE whenever the value of B2 (Quantity in Kg) is greater than or equal to 2.
- Hence, this IF formula will return 90% if the Quantity (B2) is greater than or equal to 2, or return 100% if the Quantity (B2) is less than 2.
- This calculates the applicable rate due to discount based on the Quantity entered in Cell B2.
- This IF expression is multiplied by the Quantity and Rate of apples which returns the effective total price of the apples.
- Therefore, automatically, a discount of 10% gets applied by multiplying the price

(B2*D2) by 90% if the Quantity (B2) is greater than or equal to 2.

USING THE **NESTED "IF"** FUNCTION

- In the above example, let us assume, that the store has added an additional 15% discount if the quantity exceeds 5 Kilos.
- In this case the revised formula in Cell E2 will become:

Cell E2:
=B2*D2*IF(B2>=5,75%,(IF(B2>=2,90%,100%)))

The picture below shows a logical explanation of the Nested IF formula
IF(B2>=5,75%,(IF(B2>=2,90%,100%)))

(A)	RETURN 75% IF (A) IS TRUE	(C)	IS THE QTY < 5Kg, BUT >=2Kg	(E)	RETURN 100% IF (D) IS FALSE
IF(B2>=5 ,	**75%,**	**(IF**	**(B2>=2,**	**90%,**	**100%)))**
IS THE QTY >= 5Kg?	(B)	GET INTO SECOND LOOP IF (A) IS FALSE	(D)	RETURN 90% IF (D) IS TRUE	(F)

The Table below displays an outcome of the resultant excel sheet.

Item	Qty (Kg)	Discount Applicable? (Yes/No)	Rate ($)	Total
APPLES PREMIUM	5	Yes	$3.00	$11.25

USING THE "AND" FUNCTION

AND is a logical function which returns a TRUE value only if all its components are TRUE.

For Example:

Let us assume the values in cells as B2=2, B3=3, B4=4 as per the Excel screenshot below.

	A	B
1	Variable	Value
2	X	2
3	Y	3
4	Z	4

The expression **=AND(B2=2,B3=3,B4=4)** will return TRUE because all of its component formulas are TRUE.

However, the expression **=AND(B2=1,B3=3,B4=4)** will return a FALSE because the first component (B2=1) returns a FALSE because its actual value is 2.

USING THE "OR" FUNCTION

OR is a logical function which returns a TRUE if any of its components return TRUE.

Let us utilize the same example used for AND Function.

The expression **=OR(B2=2,B3=2,B4=3)** will return TRUE because its first component (B2) returns TRUE even though all the other components return FALSE.

However, the expression **=OR(B2=1,B3=2,B4=3)** will return a FALSE because all its components return a FALSE.

CHAPTER 05
USEFUL MATHEMATICAL FUNCTIONS

USEFUL MATHEMATICAL FUNCTIONS

There are several mathematical functions, however **SUMIF** and **COUNTIF** are the two most commonly used mathematical functions. In this chapter, we will learn how to use these two functions.

USING THE "SUMIF/SUMIFS" FUNCTIONS

Let use the sample table given in the picture to understand how the SUMIF/SUMIFS functions work.

- If we want to calculate the sum of a field based on some criteria given in another field, we can use the SUMIF function.
- For cases, where we have multiple criteria, we can use SUMIFS.
- We can make use of the same table which we used for Data Filters which presents the Quantity of Apples and Oranges exported by ABC Corp. in 2016 and 2017.

A	B	C	D	E
Sr. No.	Item	Quantity	Year	Quarter
1	Apple	10000	2016	Jan-Mar
2	Orange	5000	2016	Jan-Mar
3	Apple	14000	2016	Apr-Jun
4	Orange	7000	2016	Apr-Jun
5	Apple	13000	2016	Jul-Sep
6	Orange	6000	2016	Jul-Sep
7	Apple	9000	2016	Oct-Dec
8	Orange	4000	2016	Oct-Dec
9	Apple	9000	2017	Jan-Mar
10	Orange	6000	2017	Jan-Mar
11	Apple	13000	2017	Apr-Jun
12	Orange	8000	2017	Apr-Jun
13	Apple	12000	2017	Jul-Sep
14	Orange	7000	2017	Jul-Sep
15	Apple	10000	2017	Oct-Dec
16	Orange	5000	2017	Oct-Dec

- If we were to calculate the sum of all the apple exports for both the years, then we can use the formula as:

(A)	Criteria which needs to be met	(C)
SUMIF(BB,	"Apple",	CC)
Criteria Range (Item Field)	(B)	Column (Quantity) which needs to be added when the Criteria is met

- If we had to add export quantities for apples for a particular year, say 2016, then this requires the use of SUMIFS as we have more than one criteria. The formula becomes:

(A)	Range for First Criteria	(C)	Range for Second Criteria	(E)
SUMIFS (CC,	BB,	"Apple",	DD,	2016
Sum Range which will be added once all the following Criteria are met	(B)	First Criteria which needs to be met	(D)	Second Criteria which needs to be met

Similarly, if we add as many criteria as we like.

USING THE "COUNTIF/COUNTIFS" FUNCTIONS

COUNTIF or **COUNTIFS** function is a very useful function when you want to count the number of instances by which the criteria is met.

- Utilizing the same example of ABC Corp., what if we were to identify how many quarters did the sales of any fruit was 7,000 or over.

	A	B	C	D	E
	Sr. No.	Item	Quantity	Year	Quarter
	1	Apple	10000	2016	Jan-Mar
	2	Orange	5000	2016	Jan-Mar
	3	Apple	14000	2016	Apr-Jun
	4	Orange	7000	2016	Apr-Jun
	5	Apple	13000	2016	Jul-Sep
	6	Orange	6000	2016	Jul-Sep
	7	Apple	9000	2016	Oct-Dec
	8	Orange	4000	2016	Oct-Dec
	9	Apple	9000	2017	Jan-Mar
	10	Orange	6000	2017	Jan-Mar
	11	Apple	13000	2017	Apr-Jun
	12	Orange	8000	2017	Apr-Jun
	13	Apple	12000	2017	Jul-Sep
	14	Orange	7000	2017	Jul-Sep
	15	Apple	10000	2017	Oct-Dec
	16	Orange	5000	2017	Oct-Dec

- We can use the following formula to get this value.

=COUNTIF("$C:$C, ">=7000)

The following picture explains the **COUNTIF** formula in detail.

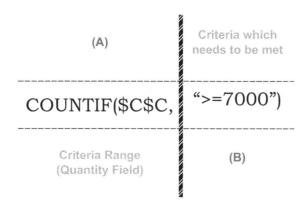

Similarly, if we were to identify how many quarters did the sales of Apple was 7,000 or over, we can use the following formula.

(A)	First Criteria which needs to be met	(C)	Second Criteria which needs to be met
COUNTIFS (CC,	">=7000",	BB,	"Apple")
Range for First Criteria	(B)	Range for Second Criteria	(D)

[52]

CHAPTER 06
USEFUL ERROR CHECKING FUNCTIONS

USEFUL ERROR CHECKING FUNCTIONS

Error checking functions are very useful to keep a check on the type of data present in a cell or expression.

We can also keep a check if the formula computes into an error.

Let us go through these functions one by one.

USING THE "ISTEXT/ISNUMBER" FUNCTIONS

The ISTEXT function checks whether the value is a text or not and returns a Boolean expression accordingly.

ISTEXT("This is a Text")	ISTEXT(123)
Checks if the value in the brackets contains Text or not. In this case, it will return a TRUE	In this case, ISTEXT will return a FALSE

- Similarly, the **ISNUMBER** function checks whether the value is a number of not and returns a Boolean expression accordingly.

- Let us take a look at the formulas below utilizing the same values used for **ISTEXT** function.

ISNUMBER ("This is a Text")	ISNUMBER(123)
Checks if the value in the brackets contains is a Number or not. In this case, it will return a FALSE	In this case, ISNUMBER will return a TRUE

- Please note the difference between both the functions.
- The **ISTEXT** function returns a TRUE if text is present anywhere in the value, whereas, the **ISNUMBER** function will return a TRUE only if the complete value is nothing but a number.

USING THE "ISERROR/IFERROR" FUNCTIONS

ISERROR function is used to return a Boolean value if the formula given returns any type of error.

ISERROR(100/0)	ISERROR(100/20)
In this case, it returns a TRUE because (100/0) computes to a #DIV/0! Error	In this case, it returns a FALSE because (100/20) computes to 5 which is a valid result

- The **IFERROR** function is also used to check if the formula returns an error or not, but it has an additional feature.
- It returns a specified value if the formula returns an error but it returns the value of the formula if it is valid.

IFERROR(100/20,0)	ISERROR(100/0,0)
Formula is valid and hence IFERROR returns 5 which is the result of the formula	Formula is invalid as 100/0 returns #DIV/0! Error. Hence, the IFERROR returns the value 0 which is mentioned in the second parameter of the formula

ISERR function is exactly the same as **ISERROR**, except that it ignores the #NA.

- If you need to trap the #NA error specifically, you can use the **ISNA** function.

ISERR(100/0)	ISERROR(100/20)
In this case, ISERR will return TRUE because 100/0 results in #NA error	In this case, ISERR will return FALSE as 100/20 computes to valid result, i.e., 5

- Let us use **ISERR** function as part of **IF** loop in the example below.

IF(ISERR(100/0),"Error","No Error")

(100/0) Computes to #DIV/0! And results in ISERR returning TRUE. Hence, the IF function returns the text Ërror

- **ISNA** function is used when you specifically want to trap the #NA error.
- Let us take an example of the **ISNA** function used to capture error from **VLOOKUP** function.

=ISNA(VLOOKUP("Apples",$B:$B,1,0))

- The VLOOKUP function searches for the text "Apples" in Column B.
- Let us assume that the text Apple is not present in the Column B.
- Accordingly, the VLOOKUP function will return #NA error, which causes the ISNA function returns TRUE.

CHAPTER 07
DATE AND TIME FUNCTIONS

DATE AND TIME FUNCTIONS

Data and time functions are a vital aspect while working on date or time specific reports.

USING THE "NOW" FUNCTION

NOW function is used to capture the current date and time. This function is most commonly used to analyze ageing related data. This formula does not have any parameter. For example: **=NOW()**

USING THE "DAY/MONTH/YEAR" FUNCTIONS

The **DAY**, **MONTH** and **YEAR** functions are used to extract the respective parameter from a given date.

Example: Let us assume that the Cell A1 in contains the Date **"5/7/2018 1:09"** which is in MM/MM/YYYY format.

=DAY(A1) function will return value 7.

=MONTH(A1) function will return value 5.

=YEAR(A1) function will return value 2018.

USING THE "HOUR/MINUTE" FUNCTIONS

HOUR and **MINUTE** functions are used to extract the respective parameter from a given date or time.

Utilizing the same example as above where Cell A1 contains the date "5/7/2018 1:09" in MM/MM/YYYY format.

=HOUR(A1) function will return value 1

=MINUTE(A1) function will return value 9

DATE/TIME FUNCTIONS

The **DATE** function is used to construct a date value based on individual parameters.

Syntax: **DATE(Year, Month, Day)**

Example:

=DATE(2018,5,7) will return a date value of "5/7/2018".

The **TIME** function is used to construct a time value based on individual parameters.

Syntax: **TIME(Hour, Minute, Second)**

Example:

=TIME(22,23,45) will return the value "10:23:45 PM".

CHAPTER 08
CUSTOM CELL FORMATTING

CUSTOM CELL FORMATTING

There are situations requiring formatting of the cells in a certain way which are not available in the standard options.

For Example:

We want to format a column containing numbers as (xxxx.xx).

- This is a simple decimal format and can be achieved by selecting the cells to be formatted
- Choose the "Format Cells" option on right-click, go to "Number" Tab.
- In the "Number" Tab, select "Number" option under "Category" field and choose the number of decimals you want
- Finally, Click Okay.

Suppose, if you want to format the number into phone number format because that is what the column is expected to contain. In such a case, we require the Custom Cell Formats.

To Enable Custom Cell Formats:

- Select the cells to be formatted, choose the "Format Cells" option on right-click, go to "Custom" Tab.

- In the "Type" field, enter the format "(000)-000-0000" as shown in the screenshot below.
- The resultant will format a number 1234567890 into format (123)-456-7890.

BEFORE	AFTER
1234567890	(123) 456-7890

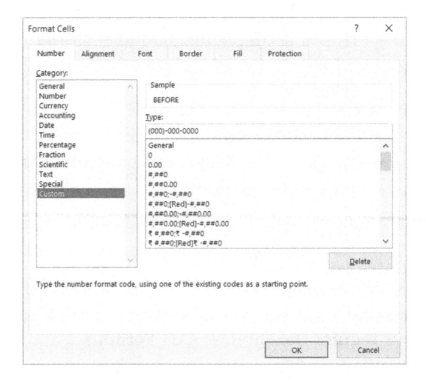

Another area which we use commonly is for date and time. We may have a requirement of displaying either date or time from a field containing both.

Let us take an example of a date entered as "5/11/2018   12:02:15 PM" (which is in the "d/m/yyyy hh:mm:ss AM/PM" format), which needs to be displayed in the year-month-date order.

- For this we can choose to enter either "yyyy-mm-dd" or "yyyy-m-d."
- The difference between the two is that the first one prefixes a zero digit to single digit numbers for month and date.
- So output for both will be "2018-11-05" and "2018-11-5" respectively.
- Notice the difference in which the date (single digit) is displayed in both the cases.

Original Format	5/11/2018 12:02:15 PM
Version 1 (yyyy-mm-dd)	2018-05-12
Version 2 (yyyy-m-d)	2018-5-13

Similarly, if we want to extract the timing:

- We can use keywords "hh:mm:ss", "h:m:s" and "hh:mm" to display the formats "12:02:15", "12:2:15" and "12:02" respectively.

Original Format	5/11/2018 12:02:15 PM
Version 1 (hh:mm:ss)	12:02:15
Version 2 (h:m:s)	12:2:15
Version 3 (hh:mm)	12:02

CHAPTER 09
CELL REFERENCING
&
FORMULA MOVES

We commonly come across occasions when we need to replicate a formula throughout the column.

As we click and drag the formula to spread it across a column, you may notice that the row numbers change in the formula with change in each row.

This is the default behavior of referencing known as **Relative referencing**.

Student Name	Marks Out of 40	Percentage (%)
Max	38	95.00
Tabetha	39	97.50
Shaun	34	85.00

Student Name	Marks Out of 40	Percentage (%)
Max	38	=B2/40*100
Tabetha	39	=B3/40*100
Shaun	34	=B4/40*100

The picture above shows an example of formula propagation in which the cell reference changes for B column, i.e. B2, B3 and B4.

- There may be cases when you may want to fix row numbers for some of the parameters in the formula.

- To enable this, we need to convert these parameters to Fixed Referencing by prefixing the dollar ($) sign to the column name and/or the row number.

Let us take an example of a Grocery Calculator which an owner uses to estimate the revenue after sales.

- The picture below shows how we use the dollar ($) sign in Column E to create Fixed referencing to the cell B1 which contains the Tax Rate.
- In future, whenever there is change in Tax rate, all the shopkeeper needs to do is to change the value in the cell B1 and the values will get automatically calculated.

Tax %		5%	
Item	Quantity	Unit Price	Total (Incl Tax)
Apple	5	$ 3.00	$ 15.75
Orange	4	$ 5.00	$ 21.00
Banana	6	$ 1.00	$ 6.30

Tax %	0.05		
Item	Quantity	Unit Price	Total (Incl Tax)
Apple	5	3	=F12*G12*(1+$F$9)
Orange	4	5	=F13*G13*(1+$F$9)
Banana	6	1	=F14*G14*(1+$F$9)

CHAPTER 10
USING VLOOKUP / HLOOKUP

USING VLOOKUP/HLOOKUP

VLOOKUP and **HLOOKUP** functions are used when you want to reference a value from a table based on match of a value in another column.

- In **VLOOKUP**, the search value is referenced across the first column of the table, as a top down approach, and a value is returned from the same row based on the column_index_number (abbreviated as col_index_num).
- In a **HLOOKUP**, the search value is referenced across the top row of the table, as a left to right approach, and a value is returned from the same column based on the row_index_number (abbreviated as row_index_num).

USING THE "VLOOKUP" FUNCTION

As mentioned above, in **VLOOKUP,** the search value is referenced across the first column of the table, as a top down approach, and a value is returned from the same row based on the Column_index_number (abbreviated as col_index_num).

The following picture describes the syntax of **VLOOKUP** in detail.

(A)	Table in which the reference value (A) needs to be searched	(C)	This number (0 or 1) is used to check if Exact match is required or not. Use 0 (FALSE) for Exact match
VLOOKUP (lookup_va lue,	table_ar ray	col_index_ num	[range_look up])
Reference value which needs to be looked up	(B)	This number is used to identify the Column index in the Table Array (B), from which the value needs to be returned	(D)

Example 1: Using the same example from Conditional Formatting chapter, the following table displays the scores of five students in the subject of Science.

	A	B	C
1	Sr. No.	Name	Marks
2	1	Max	85
3	2	Tabetha	75
4	3	Bill	95
5	4	Susan	59
6	5	Mary	64

If we have to find out the marks secured by Max, then the following formula applies.

=VLOOKUP("Max", $B$1:$C$6,2,0)

Example 2: Let us take another example where we have to reference a value between two tables, one containing the same marks of students in the subject of Science, while the other table contains the marks in the English subject.

	A	B	C	D	E	F	G	H
1	Sr. No.	Name	Science	English		Sr. No.	Name	English
2	1	Max	85			1	Max	88
3	2	Tabetha	75			2	Tabetha	79
4	3	Bill	95			3	Bill	89
5	4	Susan	59			4	Susan	77
6	5	Mary	64			5	Mary	68

- We can merge the two tables by transferring the marks secured by students in the English subject from the second table to the first table in Column D, alongside the marks secured in the subject of Science.
- The following picture describes the formula used in Cell D2 to enable this. The same

formula can be easily replicated using a simple Click and Drag from Cell D2 to D6.

(A)	Select the values in Column G (Student Name) and H (Marks in English) from the Table 2	(C)	The number 0 will return value from Column H based on the exact match (due to 0 which stands for FALSE, meaning exact match) in Column G
VLOOK UP (B2,	$G$2:$H$6,	2,	0)
Reference value which needs to be looked up (Name of the Student) **(B)**		This specified the position of the Column from the Table selected in (B) which needs to be returned. Here 1 and 2 will return corresponding values from Columns G and H respectively **(D)**	

- The Table below shows the formulas used in each of the entries. Please note the different uses of between the relative and fixed references to propagate a formula.

	A	B	C	D	E	F	G	H
1	Sr. No.	Name	Science	English		Sr. No.	Name	English
2	1	Max	85	=VLOOKUP(B2,$G$2:$H$6,2,0)		1	Max	88
3	2	Tabetha	75	=VLOOKUP(B3,$G$2:$H$6,2,0)		2	Tabetha	79
4	3	Bill	95	=VLOOKUP(B4,$G$2:$H$6,2,0)		3	Bill	89
5	4	Susan	59	=VLOOKUP(B5,$G$2:$H$6,2,0)		4	Susan	77
6	5	Mary	64	=VLOOKUP(B6,$G$2:$H$6,2,0)		5	Mary	68

USING THE "HLOOKUP" FUNCTION

In a **HLOOKUP**, the search value is referenced across the top row of the table, as a left to right approach, and a value is returned from the same column based on the row_index_number (abbreviated as row_index_num).

The following picture describes the syntax of **VLOOKUP** in detail.

(A)	Table in which the reference value (A) needs to be searched	(C)	This number (0 or 1) is used to check if Exact match is required or not. Use 0 (FALSE) for Exact match
HLOOKUP (lookup_va lue,	table_ar ray	row_index_ num	[range_loo kup])
Reference value which needs to be looked up	(B)	This number is used to identify the Row index in the Table Array (B), from which the value needs to be returned	(D)

Example 1: What if the example from **VLOOKUP** was presented as transposed table like the one below? How will we be able to fill the marks in English from the second table to the third row of the first table?

Name	Max	Tabetha	Bill	Susan	Mary
Science	85	75	95	59	64
English					

Name	Max	Tabetha	Bill	Susan	Mary
English	88	79	89	77	68

- In this case, we need to search for name across the Top Row and return corresponding marks in English from the second row of the second Table.
- You can achieve this by using the **HLOOKUP** function which is exactly meant for this purpose.
- The following picture describes the formula used in cell B3 to enable this. The same formula can be easily replicated using a simple Click and Drag from Cell B3 to F3.

(A)	Select the values in Rows 5 (Student Name) and 6 (Marks in English) from the Table 2	(C)	The number 0 will return value from Row 6 based on the exact match (due to 0 which stands for FALSE, meaning exact match) in Row 5
HLOOKUP (B1,	$B$5:$F$6,	2,	0)
Reference value which needs to be looked up (Name of the Student)	(B)	This specified the position of the Row from the Table selected in (B) which needs to be returned. Here 1 and 2 will return corresponding values from Rows 5 and 6 respectively	(D)

● Regular practice is recommended for **VLOOKUP** and **HLOOKUP** as these formulas are sometimes a bit tricky to use but are great tools once you get used to them.

BONUS CHAPTER
SHORTCUTS GOOD TO KNOW!!!

GOOD TO KNOW SHORTCUTS!

An Excel book can never be complete without a separate section for shortcuts!

ACTION	SHORTCUT	ACTION	SHORTCUT
Move To Next Worksheet	Ctrl + Page Up	Toggle Formula Display	Ctrl + `
Move To Previous Worksheet	Ctrl + Page Down	Open Format Cells Dialog Box	Ctrl + 1
Edit A Cell	F2	Merge Cells	Alt + H + M
Enter A New Line Within A Cell	Alt + Enter (while editing a cell)	Data Sorting	ALT+D => S
Copy Cell/Formula From Above	Ctrl + D	Toggle Filter (Ver1)	ALT+D => F => F
Apply Strikethrough	Ctrl + 5	Toggle Filter (Ver2)	Ctrl + Shift + L
Cancel An Entry	ESC	Freeze Pane Toggle	Alt + W + F + F
Select Entire Row	Shift + SPACE	Add Sum At Bottom Of A Column	ALT + =
Select Entire Column	Ctrl + SPACE	Current Date	Ctrl + ;
Select All	Ctrl + A	Current Time	Ctrl + Shift + ;
Select Entire Sheet	(Ctrl + A) x 2 (Twice)	Hide A Row	Ctrl + 9
Select The Next Right Cell	Tab	Hide A Column	Ctrl + 0
Select The Previous Left Cell	Shift + Tab	Insert Hyperlink	Ctrl + K

www.ingramcontent.com/pod-product-compliance
Lightning Source LLC
LaVergne TN
LVHW092343060326
832902LV00008B/779